Home from Home

Rosemary Argente

Rosemary Argente

24/10/16

First edition 2016

Printed and bound in the United Kingdom by Solway Print Tel: 01387 262960

Cover: Le Mans Crescent, Bolton
          photograph by courtesy of Bolton Council

ISBN: 978-09557327-0-6

Publishers: Asimanyi Books

www.asimanyi.books.co.uk

Books by same author:

From Blantyre to Blantyre
The Veil
The Promised Land
Home From Home
Praying Mantis
Difference
Share the Ride
Farewell Sophomore
All Mine to Have

Booklets:
Caesar and Mapanga Homestead
Journey of Discovery
Enduring Fountain – Health and Well-being
Little Book of Essays
Little Book of Poetry
Katherine of the Wheel
The Place Beyond

ACKNOWLEDGEMENTS

My thanks are due to the Bolton History Library for allowing me access to the history records of the Bolton Market and general; Jackie Casey, General Manager of the Bolton Market, for her permission and help to include Bolton Market and other Bolton Council personnel for help in general; John Bates for update on past and modern Bolton Market; Donna Karim and Zharaa, her daughter, for taking photographs of the Market stalls and much help in obtaining other information; the Author, J Frederick Horridge of the Turton Local History Society on Publication No 22; and to other persons too numerous to mention for information supplied.

The people who are mentioned in this book were not the only people I had the pleasure of knowing in Bolton, there were also many others. For various reasons, personal and otherwise, it was not possible to obtain and complete information for inclusion in this book.

I give my special thanks to the people who appear in this book for supplying information and photographs on their personal connection with Bolton – they too have written this book.

I have tried, as a true historian would, to give facts without fear or favour, and above all, without prejudice.

I CALLED AT THE GARAGE ("my garage") to replace the rear tyre of my car. Only the week before the left front tyre had been replaced. The Garage Manager could not resist:
"What is it about you and flat tyres?"
Indeed, what was it? A premonition, perhaps? I was soon to discover that at last it had caught up with me (or was it me who had caught up with it?) – that mysterious milestone just around the corner that catches up with us for so long as the sun rises and sets. I am not complaining, for I had enjoyed a good share of the agility of youth up to the age of 80 plus, and sixteen years of that in Bolton...

****

WHEREVER I CHOOSE TO LIVE, my first port of call is the market place, the grass roots of any town - after sorting out mobility problems, of course! It was 1998 when I was pleasantly surprised to discover a unique greengrocer, where I found things like yams, cassava, sweet potato, pumpkin, amaranthus (a kind of spinach, good for keeping anaemia at bay), even okra, lady's fingers! and numerous other exotic foods. It was the stall of Bates and the phrase *"merchant prince"* conjured up in my mind. I was home from home! (See booklet *Enduring Fountain*.)

****

I WAS ONLY FOURTEEN when I had so wanted to be an apprentice mechanic in my father's garage, where since I was a toddler many apprentices were trained as motor mechanics (that was in Malawi a long time ago), but I was not allowed to go to the garage let alone become an apprentice! The reason? Men were indulging in expletives in the garage. (Nonetheless, my father compensated me by teaching and allowing me to do the accounts of his business up to 'trial balance'. He brought the books home, of course!) Others of us at some point in our lives get wild ideas. To this day I have not come across a female mechanic. I was once told by a mechanic that there was one woman mechanic in the place where he worked but she was hounded out by jokes which could not be told in polite company.

What personally touched me in Bolton, aside from many other things and people, was something on the historical aspect of the place (I am a passionate historian) on two particular places on 'mills': Hardy Mill Road in Harwood, and Mill Industrial Estate, names suggestive of mill power. History tells its own story about names with 'mill' in them. One gets the impression of a motivating power, such as wind; water including power of the tide in coastal areas, fast-running water, rivers or streams, in tandem with different kinds of manufacturing processes. [Also, a name that has "chester" in it, echoes Roman administration of Britannia, former Britain.]

There are many places of interest around Bolton that share the beautiful green scenery of most of Britain, places I have seen while sitting behind the wheel. I was driving around and I found myself in a place known as Harwood when I realised that my tyre was going flat (the initial flat tyre!). I would have to call the Breakdown Service but when I looked across the road there was a garage a few yards from where I was. It was Hardy Mill Service Station. My tyre was repaired and I was on my way.

Soon after the tyre incident, my car was due for an MOT and I went back to Hardy Mill Service Station but this time it was under new ownership and management. This garage brought back memories of 'home'. There was something about it that reminded me of my father's garage: informal and yet efficient. I usually avoid taking coffee from machines but I was welcomed by a lovely young woman: with the best cup of coffee I ever tasted from a machine:

> She gave the place a gentle feminine touch
> Amid the activity of mechanics and tools.
> Her eyes...they shone like diamonds,
> But diamonds are cold...
> Hers were bluey-grey like warm pools
> Within them the shine of diamonds.
> ********

1

BOLTON IS NOTED AS A FORMER MILL TOWN and had been a production centre for textiles since Flemish weavers settled in the area dating from 1251 when they introduced manufacture of woollen cloth; and in the development of a wool and cotton weaving tradition. More Flemish weavers, fleeing the Huguenot persecutions of France settled in Bolton in the 17th century. The earliest mills were situated by the streams and rivers as at Barrow Bridge. They wove fusian, a rough cloth made of a mixture of linen and cotton.

The Huguenots were French Protestants most of whom eventually came to follow the teachings of John Calvin, and who, due to religious persecution, were forced to flee France to other countries in the sixteenth and seventeenth centuries. Some remained, practising their Faith in secret. By 1929 there were 216 cotton mills and 26 bleaching and dyeing works when Bolton became one of the largest and most productive centres of cotton spinning in the world. After World War One the British cotton industry declined sharply. One of the mills was Courtaulds who manufactured quality spun yarns in Swan Lane Mill, Great Lever, Bolton. The mill was bought by Shiloh Brothers in the 1980s. Because of the economic climate it was closed down in the late 1980-early 1990s (see chapter 8, on Ian Upton who worked at the mill as an engineer)
The large mill-storey mills and their chimneys that dominated Bolton's skyline, can still be seen around Bolton town today. By 1911 the textile industry in Bolton employed about 36,000 people.

Urbanisation and development of Bolton largely coincided with the introduction of textile manufacturing during the Industrial Revolution which took place from the 18th to the 19th centuries. This was the period when predominantly agrarian, rural societies in Europe and America, became industrial and urban.

Before the Industrial Revolution, which began in Britain in the late 1700s, manufacturing was often done in people's homes, termed as "cottage industry", using hand tools or basic machines. Life for the average person was difficult. People produced the bulk of their own food, clothing, furniture and tools.

Industrialisation marked a shift to powered special-purpose machinery, factories and mass production. Britain was the birth place of the Industrial Revolution due to its large deposits of coal and iron ore essential for industrialisation, also as a politically stable society as well as the world's leading colonial power. The colonies served as a source for raw materials and a market place for manufactured goods.

Besides the 'milling' aspect of Bolton, there were also developments in the iron industry which played a central role in the Industrial Revolution. In the early 18th century, Abraham Derby (1678-1717) discovered a cheaper, easier method to produce cast iron, using a coke-fuelled (as opposed to charcoal-fired) furnace. In the 1850s, British engineer Henry Bessemer (1813-1898) developed the first inexpensive process for steel mass-production.

Both iron and steel became essential materials, used to make everything from appliances, tools and machines, to ships, buildings and infrastructure.

The iron and textile industries, along with the development of the steam engine, played central roles in the Industrial Revolution, which also saw improved systems of transportation, communication and banking. While industrialisation brought about an increased volume and variety of manufactured goods and an improved standard of living for some, it also resulted in often grim employment and living conditions for the poor and working classes (so-called).

'Luddite' refers to a person who was opposed to technological change. Opposition to change was led by a man named Ned Ludd, though possibly he may have been a figure of doubtful authenticity (according to some). In the 1700s a series of innovations led to ever-increasing productivity, calling for less human energy. In 1779 Cotton spinning, weaving and the mechanisation of the textile industry by local inventors, such as Richard Arkwright. James Hargreaves (1722-1778) invented the spinning jenny ("jenny" was an early abbreviation of the word "engine"), a machine that enabled an individual to produce multiple spools of threads simultaneously. The spinning jenny was improved upon by British inventor Samuel Crompton (1753-1827), by his 'spinning mule', as well as later machines. By the time of Hargreaves' death, there were over 20,000 spinning jennies in use across Britain. Another key innovation in textiles, the power loom, which mechanized the process of weaving cloth, was developed in the 1780s by English inventor Edmund Cartwright (1743-1823).

****

THE NAME "Bolton" came from the Old English bothel and tun, meaning "settlement with a special building". The first record of the town dates from 1185 as Boelton. It was recorded as Bothelton in 1212. Bowelton in a charter granted by Henry III in 1251; Botelton in 1257; Boulton in 1288; and Bolton after 1307. The town's motto is *Supera Moras*, meaning "overcome difficulties" (or delays in Latin), and is a pun on the Bolton-super-Moras version of the name meaning literally 'Bolton on the moors'. Bolt and Tun le-Moors is merely a description of the land which surrounds Bolton, moorland.

The early name "Bolton le Moors" described the position of the town amid the low hills on the edge of the West Pennine Moors south east of Rivington Pike. Bolton lies on flat land on both sides of the steep-banked valley through which the River Croal flows in a south easterly direction towards the River Irwell.

Bolton is surrounded by several smaller towns and villages, which together form the Metropolitan Borough of Bolton, the administrative centre. Bolton has a long fascinating political, economic, and industrial history, though   awesome. Yet, the history of the people is humbling, not unlike the rest of the world. It is a town in Greater Manchester, in the North West of England, close to the Pennine Moors, about 10 miles (16 km) north west of the city of Manchester. Bolton town has a population of 139,403 and the wider metropolitan borough has a population of 262,400.

Some have claimed that Bolton is the largest town in Europe but apparently Huddersfield is the largest town in Europe.   It has a population of 146,234 compared to Bolton's (updated in February 2012). However, Bolton's population has increased by 15,749 in the last ten years. However, I have recently learned that Wigan is the largest town in Europe in terms of population, whereas Huddersfield is larger in area.

Despite the size of Bolton, it has never received 'city' status. Bolton Council is the largest employer of the area. The census paints a picture of an increasing ethnically diverse population in England and Wales, with a big population jump in the population born outside the UK over the last decade. Nationally the figure is 13 per cent. This is due to the fact of Bolton's welcoming attitude to strangers regardless of their ethnic origin.

BEFORE THE BEGINNING OF THE CIVIL WAR there was a social and economic tension between town and royalists in Lancashire. The town supported Parliament; and the royalists, land-owing gentry and aristocracy who controlled the rural areas were staunch supporters of the king. Also there existed a religious divide.

Some towns supported dissenting nonconformist movements. A Parliamentarian garrison in the town was attacked twice without success. However, on 28 May 1644 Prince Rupert's (Count Palatine of the Rhine, a noted German soldier, younger son of German prince Frederick V and Elizabeth, the eldest daughter of James 1 of England, James VI of Scotland) royalist army with troops under the command of the Earl of Derby, attacked again. This became known as the Bolton Massacre when 1,500 people died, 700 were taken prisoner, and the town was plundered.

At the end of the Third English Civil War, Derby was tried by court-martial as a traitor at Chesterton and condemned to death. His appeal to Parliament was rejected and he attempted to escape but he was recaptured by Captain Hector Schofield at Nantwich and was taken to Bolton where he reputedly spent his last hours at the Ye Olde Man and Scythe Inn, in the Bolton town. On 15 October 1651 he was beheaded near the Market Cross on Churchgate for his part in the massacre.

ON THE RELIGIOUS DIVIDE, the Puritans were a group of English Protestants in the 16th and 17th centuries, who sought to purify the Church of England from what they considered to be Roman Catholic practices. Some more extreme than others, in the dislike of the Anglican Church of England, they suspiciously regarded it as similar to Catholicism minus the Pope, and wanted it 'purified' (hence the name 'Puritans') of all such aspects as vestments and bishops.
The Puritans fought on both sides during the English Civil War. Also the Scots Puritan Presbyterians fought for the Royalists in the Third English Civil War of 1649-1651.

Christianity is the predominant faith in Bolton like most of Britain and evidence of this dates back to Saxon times of Christian churches, though there is also a good number of religious denominations other than Christian.The Unitarians were among the early dissenting congregations which eventually included Methodist, Presbyterian Baptist, Seventh Day Adventist and other denominations.
During the Victorian era over 40 churches were built though some became defunct, the church buildings demolished and put to other uses by succeeding generation of administrators. Today, the parish of Bolton-

le-Moors covers only a small area in the town centre since the 19th century prior to which it covered a much larger area divided into a number of chapelries (a community under a parish) and townships. The Bolton Parish Church is an example of the Gothic revival style built between 1866 and 1871. The first church on the same site was built in Anglo-Saxon times, rebuilt in Norman times and again the early 15th century.

St Mary's Deane, once the only church in a parish of ten townships in the hundred of Salford, is a church established in Saxon times. The current building dates from 1250 with extensions and restorations in the 19th century. St George's Church, financed by the Ainsworth family, was built between 1794 and 1796 when Little Bolton area was a separate township. Its last service was in 1975 and thereafter it was leased to Bolton Council and became a craft centre in 1994.

There are also Muslim and Hindu faith places in Bolton. The New Zakaria Mosque was the first mosque in Bolton and served the Muslim Community who arrived in Bolton from Pakistan and India in the 1960s. Hindus also settled in the town about the same time and their first place of worship was the former St Barnabas Church that was converted to a Hindu temple. All exist in peace and harmony.

2

THE DOMESDAY BOOK (a record of the "Great Survey" of much of England and parts of Wales completed in 1086 by order of King William the Conqueror, written in the Latin language) lists about 6,000 mills in England in 1086. Many kinds of mills existed in the past before the discovery that electricity could be applied to power for production; and pioneers in the application of power invented and developed the power of electricity.

This then became applicable to many kinds of manufacturing processes and to the many comforts provided by electric power that most communities enjoy today. Electricity is the most useful and convenient servant in man's existence.

According to an article in *The Bolton News,* 79-year old Yvonne Neary talks about 'her village' Harwood and how it had changed since the 1930s. She lived in Harwood from the 1930s until she moved in 1973, saw Harwood change from a village with only one main road to the built up area it is today. Starting at Bradshaw Brow, Lea Gate, and at Tollington Road, the village of Harwood began with Longsite and Hardy Mill right up to the Nab Gate. Yvonne goes on to say that:

"Local People used to refer to parts of Hardy Mill Road as Factory Brow, as many years ago a factory was sited there. I believe it burned down in 1917, but what it produced is a mystery."

Not such a mystery, as later discovered. There was a water-driven corn mill known as Hardy Corn Mill in the heart of the community of Harwood Township in the ancient Parish of Bolton-le-Moors, which gave its name to the present day Hardy Mill Road in Harwood. Booklet No 22 explains in much detail about the mills of Britain and much other information on the land, mills, productions, and relevant information on Bolton.

Water mills were mostly associated with grinding corn or grain of cereal plants such as wheat, barley, oats, and rye; also to grind snuff, mustard, gunpowder and flints. Water power was the initial source of energy that motivated the Industrial Revolution; sawing timber, forging iron, grinding minerals, spinning, weaving, and fulling textiles, printing, making paper and others.

It is estimated that there were over 10,000 such mills in Britain at one time or another. Prior to Biblical times the method of reducing the corn of cereals into meal or flour was by means of a hollowed rock in which the seeds were pounded with a hammer stone. Later this developed into saddle stones which consisted of a saucer-shaped bed-stone. The next stage was the development of a hand mill or quern which was normally operated by two women, common in Biblical times (New Testament Matthew 24:41).

It may be of interest to note that this latter method of a hand mill is carried out today in the remote villages of Africa to grind millet, the vital ingredient in the making of beer or a soft drink. The millet is usually ground by one woman and there may be only one quern shared by an entire village.

During their occupation of Britain, the Romans understood and used the principles of gearing to turn horizontal mill stones with their vertical water wheels. After they left Britain, a period of stagnation in craftsmanship ensued and commerce set in which lasted till the arrival of the Angles and Saxons. The latter adopted the construction of watermills on a large scale.

Over the centuries the mills went through stages of development, each enabled more ground corn production in less time and effort. The quern was an important advancement in that it milled the seeds by rotation of two upper of two horizontal stones and with a handle at the perimeter. The quern later progressed into a round powered mill or gin (engine) turned by an ass, ox, or slave. This developed into the water mill, then the windmill.

THE HARDY FAMILY WERE WELL ESTABLISHED in Harwood during the 1600s with over twenty entries for Hardier, Hardyer, Hardi or Hardy in the Bolton Parish, James Heaton Jnr was only seven years old when his father purchased the Hardy Corn Mill in 1676. Though the mill could have been worked by Thomas Hardy until James was experienced and old enough to take over. Hardy Corn Mill changed hands several times over the centuries.

John Thomas Scowcroft (1865-1931) moved into Rose Cottage, close to Hardy Corn Mill. He was a member of the extensive Scowcroft family stretching back to more than thirty generations and spanning over eight centuries. He was a common ancestor of John Thomas Scowcroft. John Thomas had inherited from his father the business of yeast merchants and importers about 1930, reportedly one of the oldest businesses in the Bolton District. He transferred part of the yeast business to Hardy Mill.

The original mill building was finally demolished after the roof had collapsed in 1919. John Scowcroft (1903-1974), the youngest son of John Thomas, converted what was left of the building into a garage. In 1929 he installed on the forecourt of the building the first electric petrol pumps in the Turton district. He eventually sold the building to the Mobil Oil Company, who in 1965 constructed a new petrol station.

In the latter part of 1998 Keith Fisher went into the site at Hardy Mill selling cars only and eventually he bought Hardy Mill taking over MOTs and repairs when the owner, Mike Dugdale, retired. In February 2008 Keith moved from Hardy Mill and purchased Church Wharf Garage, incorporating the two businesses. The name "Hardy Mill" became defunct, while the name "Church Wharf Garage" prevailed and today continues to operate as a family run business with emphasis on a personal service. Many customers of Church Wharf have been with the Garage for a good number of years.

Prior to this the premises changed hands several times and as such its uses somewhat evolved along with ownership. It started out as the Palace cinema, after which it became a wrestling stadium; then it changed to a Comma van workshop and parts centre, then it was purchased by Lance Dickenson who had a plant and skip hire business.

The Comma van and skip hire were two separate entities. Lance purchased the garage to repair and maintain his own vehicles, there were large ramps in the work shop for repairing trucks; then the garage was bought by Geoff Stockton who carried out truck and car MOTs and repairs.

Many people remember the old Palace Cinema. Apparently, there were almost fifty cinemas in the Bolton town centre: The Palace in Bury Old Road, which closed in 1956, ABC in Churchgate, Odeon in Ashburner Street, Palladium in Higher Bridge Street, Regent in Dean Road, Tivoli in Derby Street, to name a few. The last cinema to close in Bolton was the Lido which became The Cannon in Bradshawgate.

The original site of Church Wharf Garage was by the River Croal where barges operated from. The 'Church' bit most probably came from the Parish Church in Churchgate close by.

The popularity and success of any good business does not lie in impressive advertisements in print alone but how well customers are welcomed and the service they receive: therein lies the best advertisement. This is evidenced by the fact that Church Wharf Garage Limited has won successively the Exponentia "Master Garage" awards for 2013, 2014, and 2015 for excellence. Exponentia are a training company.

Church Wharf Garage Limited is also a member of a number of organisations: Autocare Group; Motor Industry code of practice; and Foxy Ladies, a women friendly organisation for lady drivers. The Garage is also a Member of the Best Garage Guide.

Church Wharf Garage in 2016

Left to right: Matthew Craven, Apprentice Modern Mechanic; Stuart Johnson, Motor Mechanic; Chris Gregson, MOT Tester and Motor Mechanic; Leon Faulkner, Motor Mechanic; Keith Fisher, Managing Director; Tom Fisher, Garage Manager; Matthew Stephenson, Motor Mechanic; Robert Hardy, Workshop Manager and MOT Tester; Jamie Gill, Garage Manager and Stephen Gore, MOT Tester and Motor Mechanic.

Pamela Clarke, Company Secretary

Façade Church Wharf Garage

Home from Home

3

SAMUEL CROMPTON lived and worked at Hall i' th' Wood', now a museum and art gallery. It was there he invented the 'spinning mule'. Hall i' th' Wood is a late medieval yeoman farmer's house built by Laurence Brownlow. Around 1637 it was owned by the Norris family, who added the stone west wing. In the 18th century the house was divided up into tenements.
Despite that Crompton invented the spinning mule that went on to be one of the most significant and universal spinning machines used by the textile industry, he fought to earn recognition for his ingenuity. But neither did he make his fortune from his machine.

Hall i' th' Wood, means Hall in the Wood, as spoken in the local regional English dialect. The wood from which the hall obtained its name was part of an ancient forest, mainly oak, which straddled the streams and adjacent countryside including part of Tonge. In the 19th century Hall i' th' Wood, deteriorated until in 1899 when William Hesketh Lever (Lord Liverhulme) bought, restored the dilapidated building and presented it to Bolton Council in 1900. This was in recognition of and as a memorial to Samuel Crompton for his ingenuity in the invention of the spinning mule.

William Lever was elected to Parliament in 1906, was raised as a baron in 1917 and became a viscount in 1922. "Liverhulme" was a combination of his own name and his wife's maiden name Hulme. Hall i' th' Wood is part of Bolton's 26 conservation areas which contains 700 listed buildings, many of which are in the town centre, and parkland including the Victorian Queen's Park, Leverhulme Park, and other open spaces in the surrounding area. Lever gave vast of acreages of land for public parks, schools and other amenities.
William Hesketh Lever (1851-1925) was the son of a wholesale grocer. He was born in Bolton and joined the family business when he was sixteen. He saw the 'spirit of soap' as his goal, a champion of health and

hygiene. His manufacture of Lifebuoy soap was his goal to stop cholera in Victorian England. In 1911, he established a palm plantation in the Belgian Congo on 750,000 hectares from the Belgian rulers. Jules Marchal documented in his book *Lord Leverhulme's Ghosts: Colonial Exploitation in the Congo:*
"Liverhulme set up a private kingdom reliant on the horrific Belgian system of forced labour, a program that reduced the population of the Congo by half and accounted for more deaths than the Nazi holocaust..."
This was the time after Great Britain had abolished the slave trade in the British Empire under the Slave Trade Act of 1807. Later followed by America and European powers.

Be that as it may, William Hesketh Lever turned out to be a great philanthropist. He was a benefactor to many and his home town Bolton boasts the largest park in Bolton, Queen's Park, created on land donated by him in 1914. Lever's invention on the formula of palm kernel oil, cotton seed oil, resin and tallow, which he called 'Sunlight Soap', was an immediate success and its fame spread far and wide.
His vision enabled Britain to evolve into the world's best selling germ protection soap and worldwide leader bringing better health and hygiene to billions of people. History shows us that more often than not, out of the strife of some who may be regarded as the 'sacrificial victims', they have been the means or the vehicle to the benefit of the many.

Lever Brothers was a British manufacturing company founded in 1885 by brothers William Hesketh Lever and James Darcy Lever. They merged with Blue Band and Flora margarines and other brands, trading as Unilever, and produced some of the worlds leading foods, home and personal care products which spread to other places including Africa: Uganda, Tanzania, Zimbabwe, Zambia, Mozambique and Malawi: where 'Lifebuoy' soap, in a magenta colour, was most popular as a bath soap; and 'Sunlight' soap, in avocado green, was most popular for laundry.

In Malawi, they produced Lux and Lifebuoy toilet soaps (in single bars); Sunlight soap (in bars of 10" long, to be cut by the user and single bars); margarine and other products. Lever traded first as Lever Brothers and later as Unilever, though the company became nationalised locally after its attainment of independence in 1966, under Hastings Banda, first president of Malawi. Unilever Malawi stopped production in Malawi in 2014 and their factory was closed and the building was sold. All Unilever products now marketed in Malawi by Unilever come from Kenya and South Africa.

****

BOLTON HAD BEEN THE TARGET for a number of attacks. One of the first aerial attacks in history, L21, a Zeppelin commanded by Oberteutnent Kurt Frankenburg of the Imperial German navy, dropped 21 bombs on the town, five of them on the working people area of Kirk Street, killing 13 and destroying six houses. Further attacks followed on other parts of the town including three incendiaries dropped close to the Town Hall.

Bolton also suffered the Black Death in 1623, referred to as 'pestilence' or 'plague'. The plague entered England in 1348 and had a devastating effect on the demographic and psychological shape of the British Isles, transformed their social and economic constitution for good. The Black Death swept across Europe from Asia during the 14th century and was responsible for the deaths of more than one third of Britain's population. Bolton was created a free borough in1253 when William de Ferrers, 5th Earl of Derby granted a charter, though it did not develop into a self-governing town, under the control of officials appointed by the lord of the manor. The Bolton Improvement Act 1792 established two local government bodies: Great Bolton Improvement Trustees and the Police Commissioners for the township of Bolton.

4

IN 1899 BOLTON WAS GRANTED County Borough status, became self-governing and independent from Lancashire County Council jurisdiction; and in 1898 the borough was extended further by adding the civil parishes of Breightmet, Darcy Lever, Great Lever, the rest of Halliwell, Heaton, Lostock, Middle Hulton, and the rest of Rumworth (the latter had been renamed Dean in 1894), Smithills, and Tonge plus Astley Bridge Urban District, and part of Over Hulton civil parish. As the population of Bolton had become in excess of 50,000 Bolton was constituted a county borough under the Local Government Act 1888, becoming independent of the administration of Lancashire County Council, though remaining part of that county for judicial, shrievalty and liutenancy.

The County Borough of Bolton was abolished in 1974 and became a constituent part of the Metropolitan Borough of Bolton in Greater Manchester. Under the UK system of government authority to run councils is by delegated legislation. The volume of legislation has grown considerably over the years. Often Acts of Parliament set out a general principle but allow (by making provision for delegated legislation) the detail to be changed as circumstances change. Delegated legislation (also known as secondary legislation) allows such changes to be made by means of a much simpler procedure. The legislation is delegated, usually either to a minister or to a local authority. Delegated legislation takes various forms, the most usual of which is a Statutory Instrument (SI). Statutory Instruments most commonly take the form of orders (generally giving effect to ministers' decisions) or regulations (which deal with detailed provisions).

It is difficult to speak generally about delegated legislation as it is used for a wide range of purposes and is scrutinised by Parliament in a variety of ways. However, several thousand SIs are created every year and they are just as much a part of the law of the land as an Act of

Parliament. The Courts can question whether a Minister, when issuing an SI, is using a power they have actually been delegated by an Act of Parliament, or whether the procedure laid down in the Act has been complied with, but cannot question the validity of the SI for any other reason.

THE MAYORS OF BOLTON ARE ELECTED ANNUALLY and serve a term of one year. The first Mayor for the Municipal Borough of Bolton was Charles James Darbinshire (Liberal,1838-1839). Followed by John Barrett (1888-1889) who was the last of the Municipal mayors and the first for the County Borough of Bolton (Conservative1889-1890). Followed by Doris Berry (Conservative, 1974-1975) for the Metropolitan Borough of Bolton.

Councillor Clifford Morris

Clifford Morris served as Mayor (2013-2014), during which time he had served as Chair of the local NHS Trust, and as a Non Executive Director in 2004/2005. He was elected leader of the Labour Group in 2004 and he has been actively involved in a number of services for the community of Bolton. He was first elected as Councillor for Halliwell in 1983 and has been leader of the Council from 2006 to date. He had also been actively involved as Health Commissioner for five years; as Chair for Greater Manchester Health and Wellbeing Board; he sits on the governing body of three schools; and is a committed Christian and lay preacher at a local Evangelical Church. An active member of his community, Cliff Morris has served as a Justice of the Peace for 20 years.

In 2014 the Bolton University awarded Councillor Morris an Honorary Doctorate in recognition for his outstanding contribution to the Town of Bolton. Clifford Morris has been married to Doreen for 50 years. She has been a massive support all through their married life. They have three children, six grand children and one great grandchild.

PARLIAMENTARY REPRESENTATION COMMENCED IN BOLTON under the Reform Act of 1832, when a Parliamentary Borough was established. The Metropolitan Borough Council is divided into 20 wards, each of which elects three councillors for a term of up to four years. Previously the Bolton constituency was represented by two Members of Parliament, and the parliamentary borough continued until 1950 when it was abolished and replaced with two parliamentary constituencies, Bolton East and Bolton West, each with one Member of Parliament.

In 1983 Bolton East was abolished and two new constituencies were created, Bolton North East, and Bolton South East covering most of the former Farnworth constituency. Also in 1983 there were major boundary changes to Bolton West, which took over most of the former Westhoughton constituency. In 2012 Bolton applied for city status but without success. Bolton was not isolated in this respect, as several other towns were also denied city status.

There is a Cabinet and Executive Cabinet Members that oversee the work of the Council, through four departments. The Cabinet is made up of four elected members with different areas of responsibilities. A partnership also exists between the Council and a variety of private, public and voluntary sector organisations through the Bolton Strategic Partnership.

5

BOLTON HAS BEEN AN INTRIGUING STAGE for drama, film and music. Le Mans Crescent has featured as a London street in the Jeremy Brett version of Sherlock Holmes, the supreme semiologist; and as a Russian secret service building in the late 1990s comedy *Sleepers*, featuring Nigel Havers and others.

Bolton has several theatres including the Octagon and the independent groups such as Bolton Little Theatre, and the Phoenix Theatre Company. Fred Dibnah, a Lancastrian steeplejack, was born and lived in Bolton. He became a much loved television historian of Britain's industrial past. Bill Naughton, playwright and author, was born in Ireland and brought up in Bolton from an early age.

The Bolton Symphony Orchestra performs regular concerts at the Albert Halls and Victoria Hall in the town centre. The 2008 BBC Radio3 Adult Choir of the Year and five times gold medal winning barbershop chorus, and the Cottontown Chorus is based in Bolton.

SPORTS CLUBS IN BOLTON: The most significant club is the Bolton Wanderers FC, an English Football League club formed in 1874 and for 102 years played at Burnden Club. In 1997 the club moved to the Reebok Stadium in Horwich. Bolton Wanderers lives up to its name and is world-famous – for those who travel much will find its supporters internationally.

Other clubs include North West England's largest Field Hockey Clubs, Bolton Hockey Club.

Two cricket clubs, the Bolton Cricket League and the Bolton Cricket Association; Bolton RUFC, rugby union club was formed in 1872 which operates four senior teams, including women's and junior sections.

Baseball clubs include Robots of Doom established in 2003 with adult and junior teams and Bolton Scarlets, dating back to 1938.

The Bolton Bulldogs is an American football team which plays home games at Smithills School.

Speedway racing known as Dirt Track Racing, was staged at Raikes Park in 1928.

Amir Khan became the WBA World light-weight champion on 18 July 2009 at the age of 22. Born in Bolton, He was Britain's third-youngest world champion boxer.

****

BOLTON PROVIDES a number of services to the community, which include dancing, keep fit, and numerous others also for the elderly. One most useful and enjoyable activity is the programme Get Active. Anna Roberts has been the Co-ordinator of the Get Active team since April 2007 and had been involved in setting up the programme from scratch.

Anna says it has been a great pleasure to see how the Programme has evolved over the years and how physical activity has improved the health and well-being of many individuals across Bolton.

Anna loves working with people and has always been passionate about physical activity and she has found it to be a great opportunity to be able to lead on the Get Active Programme and work with a fantastic team!

Anna Roberts, Get Active Coordinator.

Instructor Geoff Williams (left) at work

Geoff Williams, an award winning instructor, is one of the members of the Get Active team. He is the longest serving Get Active Instructor and he has become an extremely popular and recognisable face across Bolton. He teaches a variety of sessions around different venues in the Bolton area such as Adult Gym sessions and Gentle Stretch and exercise classes.

His commitment and enthusiasm for exercise, means his classes are always very well attended, and he is among the best instructors. Geoff strives to make his sessions fun and enjoyable – he is truly a real people person. Geoff is patient and takes a keen interest in every single participant in his sessions, and he gives individual attention to all members of his classes.

****

ON THE DANCE SCENE ARE QUITE A NUMBER   of dancing instructors under the auspices of the Bolton Council. One is the unforgettable Margaret (Maggie) Halliday, one of the Queens of Dance. Maggie has taught Ballroom, Latin, Sequence, Line Dancing and Salsa over the last sixty years that she has been a qualified dance teacher.

At fifteen Maggie had no wish to learn to dance but her friends persuaded her to go with them on a dance course that was just starting. Well, it ended up with her marrying the teacher! And, so her dancing life began. By the time she was eighteen she had qualified as a dance teacher. She then went on to become a Member, then a Fellow, an adjudicator and examiner for the United Kingdom Alliance and it was through them she went out to India to set up dance schools there.

She is an Associate Member and Fellow of the International Dance Teachers Association. Over time Maggie had seven dance schools in

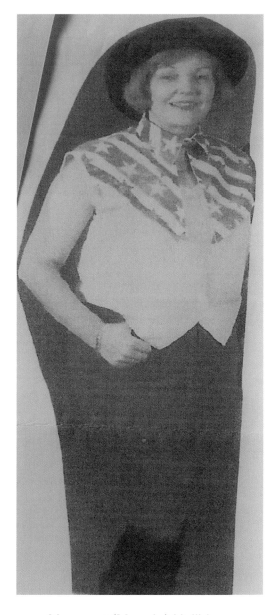

Margaret (Maggie) Halliday

Bolton and has also run dancing holidays all over the world as well as many Charity Dances. She has also put lots of students in for their medals and also trained many to become dance teachers themselves. The Bolton Council had asked Maggie to put on a Salsa dance event and she took her group to Hall i' th' Wood, where the Salsa was performed. The event was a Fun Day on 28 August 2009 to celebrate the life of Samuel Crompton, organised by Bolton at Home and the Museum of Bolton, when Hall I' th' Wood was open to the public on a guided tour.

Salsa dancers at Hall i' th' Wood

Salsa dancers at Hall i' th' Wood

Bolton News (Tuesday 05, January 2016) carried an article entitled "Quick-stepping Back in Time" featuring dance choreographer Jack Murphy and Flossie Dawson from Halliwell; also pictures of Bolton's Palais de Dance in 1974; and of Astoria Palais de Dance in Higher

Bridge Street pictured in the 1950s. which saw a boom in ballroom dancing with Mecca Dancing Limited taking over the Palais in 1956 and in October 1958. From the Astoria Palais de Dance to Icon created by local builder Thomas Bolton and first opened the doors in 1928.

The popular BBC "Come Dancing" programme was broadcast from there. It was at the heart of Bolton's social scene until taken over by discotheques and the Palais became the iconic dance spot when Cinderella Rockefeller opened in 1979, before closing in 1987. It had also been Ritzy's and later Icon before closing in January 2012.

Another Queen of Dance is Laura James. Laura teaches a variety of dance styles to children from age two up to adult. Her field also include, ballet, tap, 'cheer-leading', street dance, modern jazz, and choreography.
Laura started dancing when she was two and began to teach when she was ten. Laura was born in Bolton and she is now 32 and she opened her own dance school in 2001 She also works in communities and local schools within Bolton. She finds it exciting and inspires children to enjoy dancing (see Chapter 10).

6

MANY PERSOSNAGES FROM DIFFERENT ETHNIC backgrounds have been welcomed in Bolton, where they have been free to pursue and share their vision with the Bolton community; with much help from the Council. Nat Biney is one of the many such personages. In partnership with Bolton Council, Nat provided, and still provides, many services not only to the African community but also on a number of events involving the entire Bolton community. He is a founding member and chairman of the African Community Association of Bolton (ACAB) for the last 10 years.

Nat was born into a well respected royal family at Akuapim Larteh-Kubease in the Eastern Region of Ghana. His uncle Nana Asiedu Agyemfra V, was the longest serving chief in Ghana, 63 years at Larteh-Kubease, till 2002 when he passed away at the age of 87 years. The royal house of Nana Agyemfra is called 'Kubease Ahenfie'.
By bloodless conquest, save King Shaka Zulu's, later his successor, King Cetshewayo and his 20,000 army who defeated British invasion of Zululand at the Battle of Isandlwana (1879) in South Africa, the royal houses of Africa were recognised but reduced to chieftainships by British administration; though a few were recognised as 'kings' (see *From Blantyre to Blantyre* under Historical Information).

When Nat came to Britain in 1976 he studied for a degree in Textiles (ATI) at the Bolton Institute of Technology, which is now the Bolton University. He went on to Leeds University to read Mphil/PhD in Textiles. Sadly, due to a military coup (1966-79) in Ghana bursaries became defunct and he was unable to pursue his textile career.
Since then, Nat has served in a number of positions, private and public, as a volunteer in different capacities: as a local school governor, first elected African Councillor in his local Church, St Mary's Parish Church, Dean, Bolton (which is over 650 years old).

Besides Nat served as a Trustee board member at the Bolton CVS, Bolton Racial Equality Council, and Bolton Arts Forum. He also sits as a representative of the African communities in Bolton on Stronger Community Partnership meetings including other Community bodies with the Bolton Council. Currently he is a member of the Governing body of Achievement, Cohesion and Integration Service (ACIS) and a Trustee Board Member of Health-watch Bolton.

He became one of the pioneers and founding members of the Artists in Schools Agencies representing Bolton/Bury and Rochdale offering African arts and cultures in local schools in North West and beyond for the past twenty years. He has also held the position of chairperson of the Ghana Union of Greater Manchester.

He became the first African to be appointed by the Lord Chancellor to the Advisory Committee Panel on the Bolton Bench, a position in which he served for 9 years. Nat has served as a local Magistrate for over 17 years.

Nat is married to Levina, a beautiful, gentle woman, who was trained as a teacher in Ghana before coming to Britain. Mr and Mrs Biney have three adoring children and two grand children. Nat and Levina are kind, bubbly, respectful and as a result, they have made many friends at work and in the community.

Levina has been Nat's mentor, mother, sister, friend, and a loving and supportive partner in his life's journey. Levina worked as a quality controller at Beehive Mill for 25 years before she was made redundant; and for Morrisons for the past 9 years. Levina has been an excellent volunteer and Executive member of ACAB.

Nat and Levina Biney [2015]

Back: Nat Biney, Chairman ACAB and Flossie Gomile, Deputy Malawi
High Commissioner to Britain. Front: Author and her daughter, Lorna
Argente on the occasion of the launch of *Always With You –*
A Malawi Legacy at Victoria Hall, Bolton.
Under the auspices of ACAB and Bolton Council

Among other personaages who worked with Nat Biney on the various
activities connected with charities was Alice Burton fom Malawi. Alice
had lived in Bolton for a good number of years. She was a happy
bubbly character, always at the forefront to assist, and ready for the
extra mile. Sadly, she had lost her two grown-up sons and she decided
to return to Malawi to be near her only surviving daughter. Alice echoed
the award-winning but sad movie *Alice Doesn't Live Here Any More* as
she was greatly missed in Bolton.

Poor Alice yet suffered another sad blow when her daughter Maria died. She could not take it and passed on three months after her daughter.

Alice Burton

ALSO AMONG THE MANY PERSONAGES who live in Bolton is Donna Karim who runs a charity that builds wells for Malawi villages. She is inspired by constant thoughts about what she personally could do to give back and make a difference to another person's life.
She feels that building wells was something that could benefit so many. While we take for granted the amenity of mains water supply, there are many who do not have such a basic amenity of a water supply and a well in the remote areas of Malawi is a blessing.
Donna is assisted by her husband Marcus Karim who comes from Malawi. In total they have built five wells in Malawi, at the villages of: Chinsapo, Masoachidya, Nsudwe, Chiuzira, and Chitedze. Donna has more funds for three more wells to build at Zomba and Salima.

The Karim Family: (left to right) Zahraa, Zayn, Donna (mother), and Marcus (father)

Donna and Marcus organise annual events and have done so for the past five years with the aim to raise enough money to build one well per event, and they have succeeded in doing this. Her family are also involved in the activities: her parents, her sister and her aunt help with all the catering at the fund-raising events. Marcus takes care of the DJ aspect as well as helping to sell tickets. Their daughter, Zharaa, who has a lovely singing voice, performs and their son, Zayne, helps with various areas on the night. Donna's efforts are great not only in bringing so many people together for a good cause but also to raise necessary funds to build the wells.

One of the type of wells built around Malawi

THE BOLTON LOCAL RADIO STATION began broadcasting in 2009 as 96.5 Bolton FM. The radio station was given the name 'Tower' as a local link to both towns in the station's coverage area: Turton Tower in Bolton and Peel Tower in Holcombe Hill at Ramsbottom near Bury. Part of Tower FM is a British Independent Local Radio station and broadcasts across the towns of Bolton and Bury from its studios in Orrell, in the Metropolitan Borough of Wigan.

****

THE ROYAL BOLTON HOSPITAL is located in Farnworth. It was the day a patient was to be discharged from the Hospital after a knee replacement when the nurse said:
"We will let you go home on one condition."
"What is that?" Asked the patient.
"You must leave us your beautiful dressing gown."
"Oh! That is all I have left of him." She pleaded.
"Well, we will not let you go", The nurse persisted.
"Al right I will make a deal with you. I promise to leave it in my will for you."
Then the nurse let her go!

There were signs of under-staffing (universally apparent these days) as one's heart goes out to the nurses, who despite the odds, combine warmth and friendliness with expertise and professionalism. They never lost that compassionate 'caring touch' with a smile and a joke thrown in.

Submission to the surgeon's scalpel and the after care received from an angel physiotherapist, not only enabled one to walk normally, but also to continue dancing.

The angel gave the patient a walking stick. Did the patient use it for walking? No. Did she use it for whacking? Oh! No! She placed it across her back while dancing around in her abode to keep the 'dowager's hump' at bay. But leave that to 'Father Time' and she shall soon use it for walking!

****

OFTEN ON PUBLIC OCCASIONS   at Victoria Square one witnessed various events organised by the Bolton Council, also in Music. On one such occasion, before   approaching the Square, one could hear the sound of band music playing the British Grenadiers (an echo of 'home' where annually a local army band played at the King's Birthday Parade around countries of the British Empire).

Then one beheld a pipe band performing at the Square, magnificently accoutred in military doublets with regimental badges, tartan kilts, white hair sporrans, pristine spats and high plumed feather bonnets. These were not Scottish Highlanders but soft-eyelashed member youths of the Shree Swaminarayan Gadi Pipe Band of Bolton,   of the Hindu Swaminarayan faith, followers of Jeevanpran Shree Muktajeevan Swamibapa. They played other tunes: *Mairi's Wedding, Donald Where's Your Trousers?, Danny Boy,* and others.

This band music not only expressed the spirituality of India through the emotionalism of Scotland but also the citizenry of Bolton in the expression of great heart. Truly multicultural.

Jeevanpan Swamibapa was a Hindu monk and founder of the Swaminarayan faith – a worldwide movement dedicated to the promotion of peace and co-operation through beauty. When he visited his disciples in London in 1970, a concert was given in Trafalgar Square in his honour. Once he heard the Scottish bagpipes for the first time, he was moved to call upon his supporters to take up the bagpipes.

When we admire and take something from another culture as our own for what is not ours, and to facilitate difference and enjoy its free expressions, we do not lose ourselves in what we admire, as it only enriches us.

7

THE TOWN RECEIVED its first Charter to hold a market in Churchgate, and annual fair, granted by King Henry III in 1251. This grant included vast lands as described in the grant document: "in the Manors of Lyverpull, West Derby, Everton, Crosseby, Wavertgre, Salford, Bowelton, in the County of Lancaster..." to William de Ferrers, the Earl of Derby, to make Bolton a market town and borough on January 14 1253.

Bolton Market is located in Ashburner Street. The origin of `Ashburner' is obscure among the streets which formed the Bolton of pre-industrial revolution. In 1850 the Corporation acquired the right to construct markets under the Borough of Bolton Act 1850.

The Bolton Iron and Steel works closed in 1930, making a large area between Moor Lane and Black Horse Street. The decision to combine a Fish Market, Wholesale Market and Retail Market in one building became a reality in 1932. The structure was made from brick and stone with a slate roof in the twentieth century during the mid period of the Second World War.

Bolton, in Greater Manchester, is well-known for its produce, where 50% of its stalls now sell food and drink. Ashburner Street markets and their Environments were opened by Councillor Kearsley on 26 September 1932. In his opening ceremony he stated that:

> "It is expected that this market will become the most important one in Lancashire, apart from Manchester and Liverpool; and that it will be the greatest retail centre for miles around".

Indeed, in 2010 Bolton was declared Britain's Best Indoor Market Hall. Despite the odds presented by nearby supermarkets: Sainsbury, Morrison and Asda, the Market continued to thrive.

At the time, citrus was imported from the Mediterranean, Bananas from the Carribean (West Indies as it was known then), in quality and variety. Retailers from Westhoughton, Ramsbottom, Darwen, Chorley, and Walkden wholesale Markets rent their stalls from the Council and fit them out according to their own requirements. The licence to trade goes with the ground lease for the stall.

In the years 2012-2014 the Market was under extensive refurbishment much to the inconvenience of the public and worse for the stall owners but it was all worthwhile in the end result. Bolton Market is one of the best markets in Britain, for fresh fruit, vegetables, fresh fish, shell fish, including Tilapia. This is a fish also known as St Peter's fish which appears in the Bible (Matthew 14:13-21, New International Version): 2 fish and 5 loaves of bread which Jesus fed to the multitude.

Tilapia or St Peter's fish could be found only in two lakes of the world: Lake Galilee and Lake Malawi (the latter is located on the Great African Rift Valley; perhaps the two lakes, Galilee and Malawi, are connected underground(?). Most countries, commencing with Israel, including Europe, fish-farm Tilapia using Israeli Agricultural Technology.

Bates Brothers
John and Danny

The brothers brought, and still do, food items from many parts of the world, including some similar to those of Malawi.

Bolton Market would remind one of Shepherds Bush Market of the early 1950s, in London, where people from the Commonwealth countries found "a touch of home".

The Bates brothers commenced their greengrocery at Bolton Market in1971, prior to which, John, the elder brother, at the age of thirteen in 1960, worked for George Smith, a friend of his father and a greengrocer. At sixteen he went to sea and when he returned home, at twenty, he worked for Jackie Liptrot, a Bolton and Bury greengrocer.

From left to right: Dimple, Danny Bates, Nicola, and John Bates.

John said that there were then, at Bolton Market, 52 independent stalls: all greengrocers, mainly fruit and vegetables. The only other three were a sea food store and the other two, cooked meat stalls. There were no butchers or delicatessens then.

The Supermarkets in Bolton commenced with Lennons, Peagrams and later the big ones followed. The arrival of the big supermarkets was a blow to the Market stalls because of the aspect of supermarket "convenient" characteristic: the shoppers' preference to "One Stop" - get every-thing in one place. It may be convenient but it is not `competitive' as one may discover. But then, there is no such a thing as a free lunch!

John Hoole stocks alternative remedies, as most other things, internal and external medicinal items. He also stocks a variety of teas, vinegar, and sugar-free dried fruit. His stall is a paradise for those who wish to pay heed to health matters in their diet and generally.

Market Chippy
Peter McGowan

The façade of Peter's stall at Bolton Market

Peter McGowan lives in a strong Christian faith and by virtue of his name "Peter", he decided to trade in fish, not as a fisherman but to serve fish in the name of God. Peter does serve the most delicious fish and chips on the premises and also provides a Take Away service.

Lyndel's
Linda Halliwell

Linda has been managing her present stall for six years, but has been on and off the market for thirty years. One would be pleasantly surprised to find that amongst the great variety of delicious cakes and biscuits Linda sells, is a special fruit cake that is free from sugar.

Linda shared the information that there was no heating at the Market, and this made life rather difficult, particularly in the winter months,.

Linda Halliwell

Christine's Cheese Stall
Susanne Slater

The stall has been there for 37 years and Susanne has been at the stall for four years.

Bannisters
Steven Latham

Steven Latham, greengrocer, has been on Bolton Market for 53 years. He first joined Bannisters at the age of fifteen and later he became the owner. Steven explained that Bolton Market has changed over the years, and has become more cosmopolitan. Consequently, he found it increasingly necessary to widened the scope of variety in the commodities he sold in his attempts to ensure that he supplied everybody.

Steven Latham, proprietor

Allan Mollover, at Bannisters

Carrs Pasties
John Carr

Margaret Bird (right), manager and colleagues

Margaret has worked for Carrs Pasties for the last 20 years. John Carr commenced his pasties business 70 years ago in Haliwell, Bolton, and he opened the stall at Bolton Market in October 1996.

Home from Home

The Milano Pizza stall has been on Bolton Market for 5 months and the stall is owned by Jalal who comes from Iran. He commenced in Blackburn Road, Bolton 22 years ago and later decided to have a stall at Bolton Market. Jalal said he likes Bolton very much and he had been very busy till the last 7-8 years or so when business began to slacken slightly. He said to me: "I love the people of Bolton, they are so friendly."

Jane has had her stall for 20 years. She began in Whitby, Manchester. She said she loves 'the feel of it', handling and selling shoes which makes her happy.
She is assisted by her son, Mark. The Shoebox also stocks children's shoes.

African Cuisine
Job Alain

Job Alain, and his infectious laughter, is from Cameroon. He said that he wanted to introduce the wonder of African cuisine to Bolton Market and all the exotic atmosphere it has to offer.

Job Alain

Indeed, Alain's dishes takes one to another part of Africa. One would not expect it, but African cultures do vary around Africa, not unlike the cultures of other parts of the world, particularly in the field of cuisine.

A Taste of Sunshine
Julie Yarwood

Julie Yarwood had lived in Tenerif for fifteen years. She decided to bring back to Bolton a little bit of Tenerif where people could have friendly "chit chats." Her inspiration was to bring a taste of sunshine and give something back to Bolton. The stall has been on Bolton Market for over a year now, Julie is from Bolton and owns the stall. When she does not have the item customers want, she sends them next door. She believes and tries to live by the "spirit of friendship," as Lisa put it: "We are all friends here."

Lisa works at the stall on certain days.

Jazak Foods
Zubada and John Paul Lee

Zubada Lee, along with her husband John Paul Lee, a local English man, jointly own Jazac Foods. Zubada in her own words said:
   "I have lived in 'friendly' Bolton for eleven years."
Zubada and John have invented a mixture of Indian and Spanish dishes. They also specialise in Indian curries.
She went on to say theirs is a fast take away for the commuters to Bolton.

The Stationery Box
Joanne Crompton

Joanne Crompton has been on Bolton Market for thirty-two years now. She commenced business since she was eighteen.
The Stationery Box stall is where the shopper will find everything in the stationery line from visitors' cards to diaries.

****

Proprietor of Plantation

Mo has been on his stall for 7 years. He indicated that he preferred the old Market before it was renovated. He lives in Bury and commutes to Bolton.

Barry Archer commenced his stall at Bolton Market when he was 21 years old and he has been at the Market for 49 years. Most of his merchandise is in exquisite colourful China.

The pet stall of Mrs Evans is a paradise for pet owners, from dog collars to bones and much else in between.

Jayne has been in business for 25 years. She first commenced in flowers, then moved to shoes, and presently she specialises in bags and luggage in many styles and colours. She is a 50% owner of the stall. The shopper certainly has a great choice in bags and luggage, in many styles and colours to suit every occasion, from the little purse to the travel bag.

THE TEENAGE MARKET rather intrigued me. The event was organised by Bolton Market to give young people an opportunity to show their business ideas as well as their musical and dramatic talents.

The Teenage Market is a growing nationwide initiative set up by teenage brothers Joe and Tom Barratt in Stockport as a way to support local young people and transform town centres.

Those aged 13 to 25 years old, from Bolton, were invited to pitch for a spot at the market. The Teenage Market was located on Victoria Square, Saturday, May 21 from 10am to 4pm.The event was to take place in the Love Your Local Market fortnight – a national campaign aimed at celebrating market culture across the UK.
There were about 22 traders and 7 performers all showcasing their talents, and another teenage market was planned for September 2015.

9

A GROUP OF FIVE CHILDREN THREW MUD on the sitting room windows. The occupier retreated to the bedroom and closed the curtains. The children went to the back of the house and continued to throw mud on the bedroom window. Children can, sometimes, be intimidating. Where would they get such vindictive ideas from? We could readily say from "conditioning by their parents" but then this could be an assumption, and assumptions only make a fool out of you and I.

No place is without some unpleasant incidents. When such things occur it gives us the opportunity to understand and appreciate the value of the action taken by the appropriate authorities. The standard of reasonableness is that a community is not a barrel of apples where one or two bad ones would contaminate the lot.

At the time Bolton was policed by the Bolton Central Division of Greater Manchester Police, which covered the town centre, Rumworth and Halliwell. Astley Bridge Police Station covered Tonge and The Haulgh, Breightmet and Crompton. Great Lever and Little Lever were covered by Farnworth Police Station. Heaton, Lostock, and Smithills were covered by Horwich Police, Middlebrook.

The matter was reported to the police and a pretty police woman in her mid thirties promptly came along. She kindly listened to what had happened. The nuisance was efficiently and removed with alacrity. The Council fitted lockable gates on the entrance to the back of all the premises situated on that road.

****

A FEW WEEKS AFTER THE MUD-SLINGING INCIDENT, one morning at 7 am there was a note from the police asking the occupier to call them 'about her car'. She looked out of the window and the car was not there. The police said they had been tipped by one of the neighbours who had seen two men take the car away.

The car was found in the next street, all smashed up to a complete write off; the radio and other bits and pieces were missing. A case came before the magistrate who ordered the main culprit to pay for the damage according to his financial means. Reparation instalment cheques were issued to the owner by the magistrate's court. She never knew which of her neighbours had reported the matter to the police but her thanks came from her heart.

****

THERE WERE OTHER PLEASANT INCIDENTS in the street about a dog and one about a magpie. Sparky, the dog, lived a few houses further down at the bottom of the road with Sarah and her partner. Sparky was always up and down but one never discovered where he went to on his daily jaunts, though he was rather friendly and ready to stop for a little chat.

Sarah and partner parted and she got another partner. After a few months they parted and a new partner came along. Then there was another separation but Sparky had had enough he went along with the third partner. He was greatly missed.

The abode was graced by one tree at the front garden and two at the back in well-tended lawns. Pigeons, gulls, thrushes and other birds fed in the back garden. Like some compensation, a shy lone magpie (Mag) knocked at the sitting room window after five in the evening. The occupier gave her a slice of bread.

Routinely, when other birds had gone to roost, she came to the back kitchen window between five and six in the evening, for her supper of a slice of bread: "white if you please!" Sometimes she came to the front knocking at the window to remind the occupier about her slice of bread.

Then life went on smoothly as every place has its beauty in varying degrees. Towards the end of the eighth year something was happening to the premises, everything was getting damp, carpets were getting ruined and the situation was baffling.
On opening the gate to the back of the premises it was found that a pool of water had formed outside, dripping from the flat above. The neighbour upstairs had gone on holiday for three months and had left a tap on! Then a move was made across the main road from the damaged premises.

As the occupier was hopeless in learning bird dialogue she was unable to tell Mag that she was moving to a place just across from Tonge Moor Road so Mag could fly over for her slice of bread. Hopefully, she prayed, that some new tenant would discover Mag's needs.

10

TWO VERY SPECIAL PEOPLE organised a memorable get together for the author's 80th birthday in 2010, at the Bolton Excel Centre, Lower Bridge Street.

This was perhaps one of the last events at that venue, since soon after, the whole place was demolished to make way for new development.

Archie and Lorna

Tobias (left) and Hugo just getting ready for the party

Laura James and her sons: Tobias and Hugo

A beautiful baby – one of the guests

Helen and Ian Upton

My 24-hour caring persons in a time of illness and strife were Helen and Ian; and Helena Dias (for the latter, an affine by marriage, see *From Blantyre to Blantyre*, chapter 11, 'Brick Fields').

Bob Cameron and Helen Spencer Upton

Many people attended the party: family, friends and acquaintances, some travelled from abroad. It was truly a most memorable get-together occasion. (For Bob Cameron see *From Blantyre to Blantyre*, chapter 20, 'Definitive Journey'.)

80th Birthday

INDEED: "What was it about me and the flat tyres?" It was the third car I obtained through my garage to keep me going till I mustered enough courage to get an automatic car to suit my current condition. Throughout my driving life (71 years, 3 during the learning process to drive and 68 plus licensed years) I only ever had one automatic car, a Honda; for I have never felt that "I was driving" when I was behind the wheel of an automatic car.

It was just after the Breakdown Service had sorted out the flat tyre to enable me to go to my garage when I discovered that I was to leave behind all the good people I had known and things I had enjoyed for sixteen years.

Life is a river, like its flowing water, forever passes away...

Choice Domicile

From Scout Road down the craggy slope
To the horizon, an inverted bowl,
Soundless in semi-panoramic expanse.
Smooth, wide, long avenue of trees and grass,
Fires burning within flanking houses,
Oblivious to whatever enduring weather glass.

Shades of green darkened to solo midnight tone
Grazing horses stabled for the night,
Bleating ewes quieted by the sunset.
Hikers exhausted, departed before twilight,
Intriguing salmon pink sky,
Disappearing into midnight tone.

Her shimmering gown,
A terrestrial constellation
In place of the sun sublime in all her majesty,
Ousting the solo midnight tone,
Vying with Blackpool Lights,
This is Bolton! My Town!

Poem by author
First Published in 2008

A TRIBUTE

Raymond Halliwell

The *Bolton Evening News* (Tuesday 27 March 2001) printed an article entitled *Tribute for pioneer of racial harmony* on the late Mr Raymond Halliwell who played a vital role over 18 years as head of Bolton Racial Equality Council before retiring in 1995. He resigned as an MP so that he could devote all his time to improve race relations.

The secret of Bolton's racial harmony and peace, aside from the humanitarian aspect of the people themselves, is the local Council's involvement and inclusion of members of the whole community in public aspects, services and local events, regardless of race, creed or religion. Bolton is a *role model* for racial harmony for a peaceful existence, which echoes most welcoming areas to strangers in Britain. According to a survey of the British Association for the Advancement of Science, Boltonians are the friendliest people in Britain.